for 1000+ tutorials ... use our
free site .... drawinghowtodraw.com

DRAWING FOR KIDS

WITH CURSIVE LETTERS IN EASY STEPS ABC

CARTOONING FOR KIDS AND LEARNING HOW TO DRAW WITH THE CURSIVE ALPHABET

LETTER A DOGGY

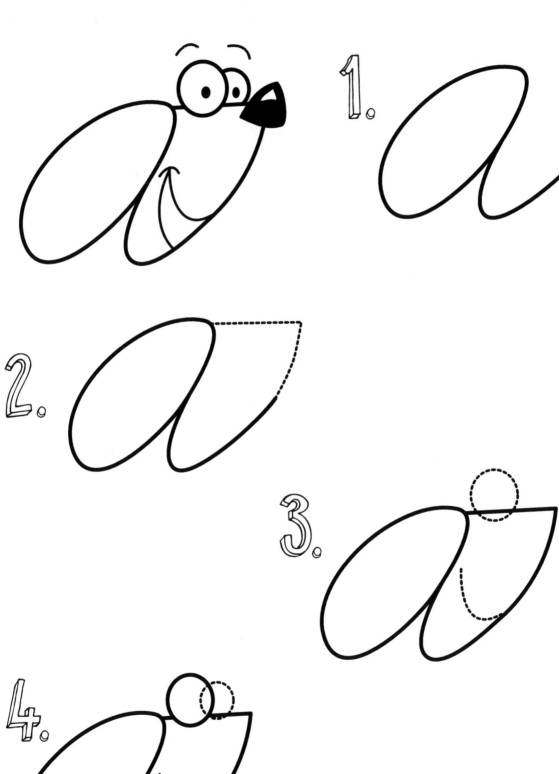

5.

↓ NOW YOU TRY ↓

LETTER B ELEPHANT

1.

2.

3.

4.

Letter C →
Shapes

5.

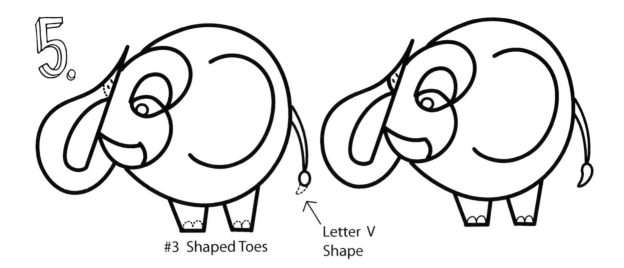

#3 Shaped Toes

Letter V Shape

↓ NOW YOU TRY ↓

LETTER C GUY

1. C

2. Letter C Face

Letter D Feet

3. Letter C Nose and Ear

4. Letter V Shape

Sideways Letter P

#3 Shaped Fingers →

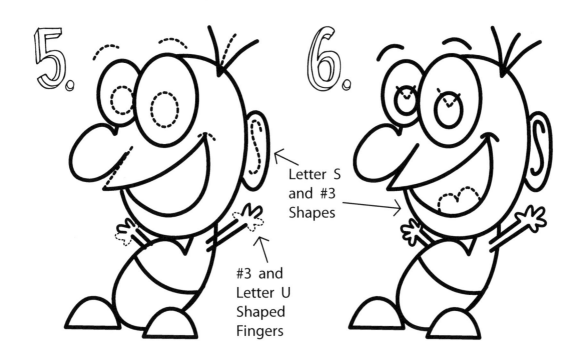

5.

Letter S
and #3
Shapes

#3 and
Letter U
Shaped
Fingers

6.

NOW YOU TRY

LETTER D BIRDIE

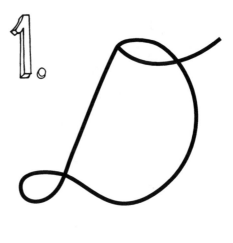

1.

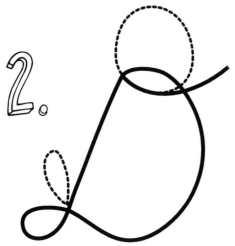

2.

Tear Drop Shapes
(Made by Drawing
a Letter U and
then Pinching
it at the Top)

3.

Letter V
Shapes

4.

Letter U
or J Shaped
Wing

↓ NOW YOU TRY ↓

LETTER E BUTTERFLY

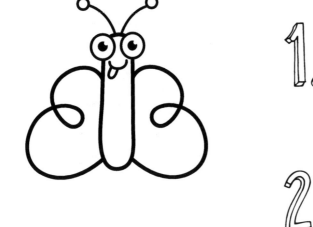

1.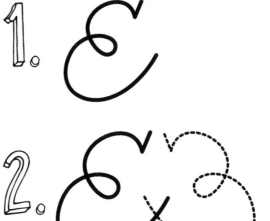

2.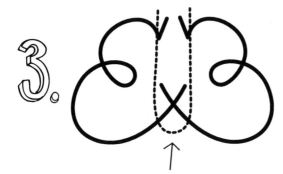

Draw the Letter E backwards now

3.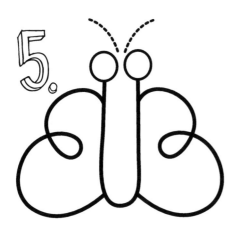

Tall Letter U Body

5.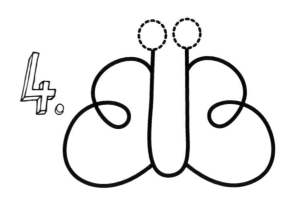

6.

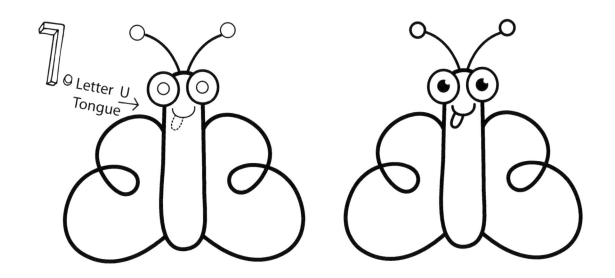

7 θ Letter U
Tongue →

↓ NOW YOU TRY ↓

LETTER F DUCKLING

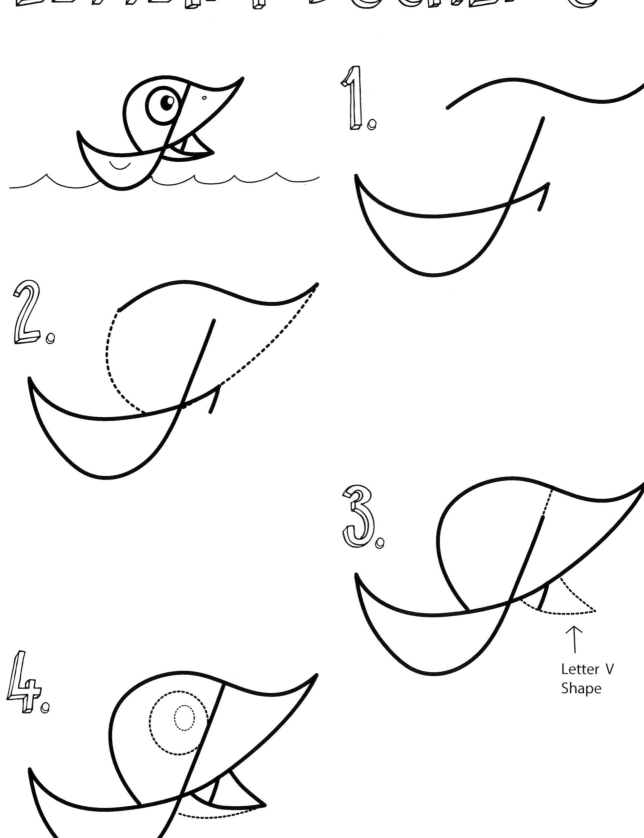

1.

2.

3.

Letter V Shape

4.

5.

↓ NOW YOU TRY ↓

LETTER G DANCER

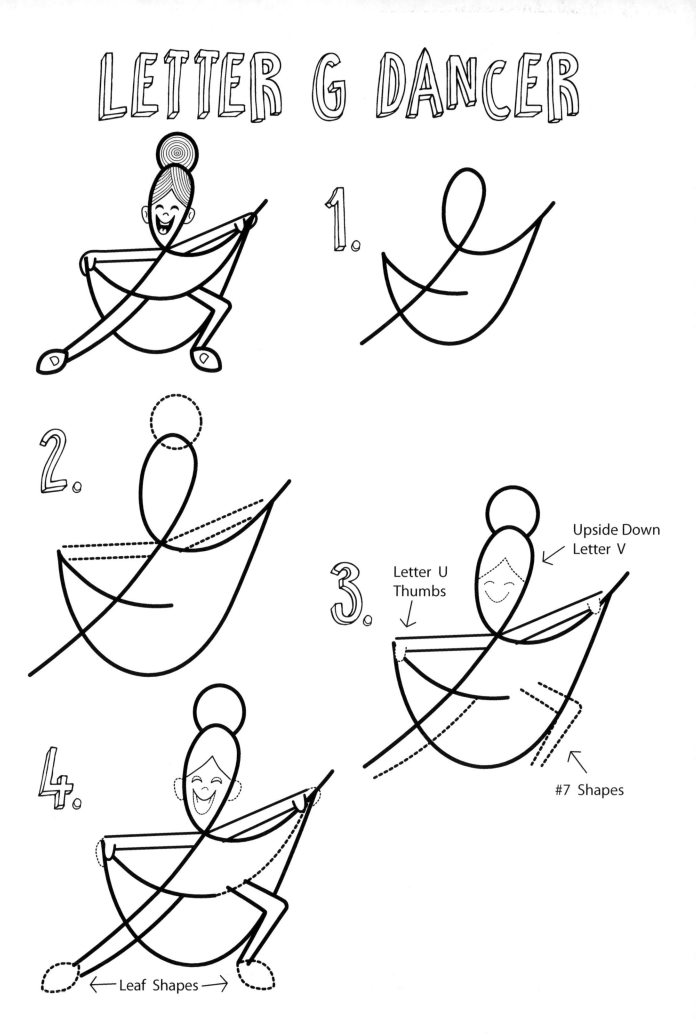

1.

2.

3. Letter U Thumbs

Upside Down Letter V

#7 Shapes

4. ← Leaf Shapes →

5.

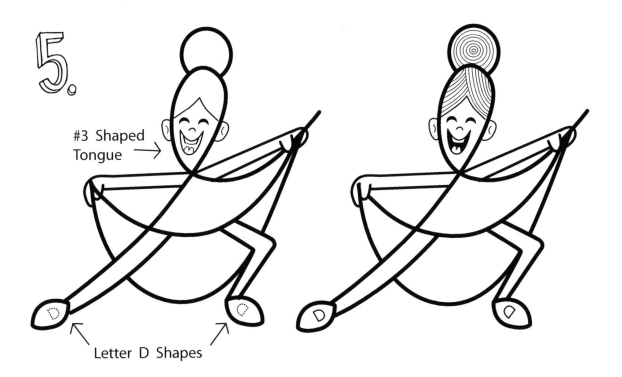

#3 Shaped Tongue

Letter D Shapes

↓ NOW YOU TRY ↓

LETTER H MOUSE

1.

2.

3.

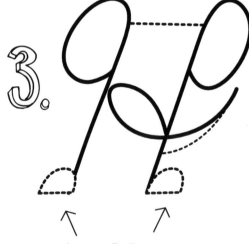

Letter D Feet

4.

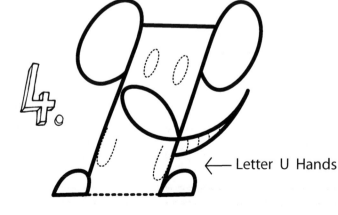

← Letter U Hands

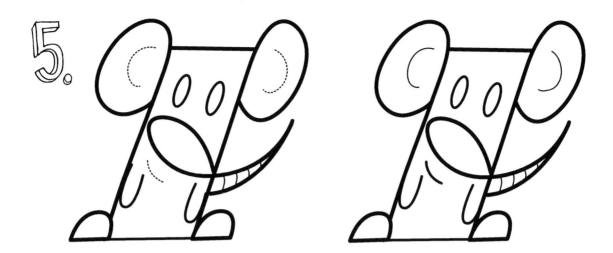

5.

↓ NOW YOU TRY ↓

LETTER 1 DOGGY

1.

2.

3.

Letter #9 and
Letter P Ears

4.

LETTER J BUGGY

1.

2.

Letter U and V
Shapes

3.

Letter V and U →
Shapes

4.

5.

↓ NOW YOU TRY ↓

LETTER K SLEEPY GUY

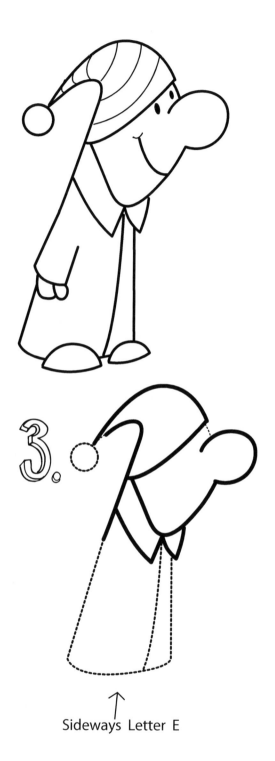

1.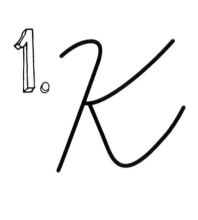

2.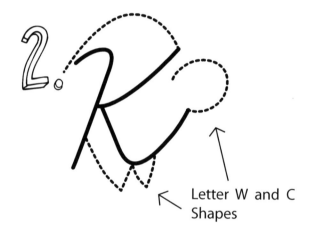
Letter W and C Shapes

3. Sideways Letter E

4.
Letter D Shapes

5.

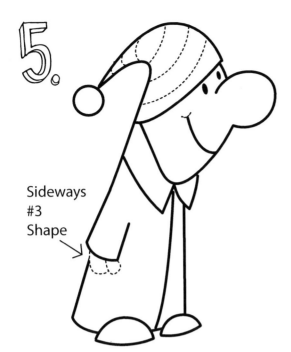

Sideways
#3
Shape

↓ NOW YOU TRY ↓

LETTER L GIRLY GIRL

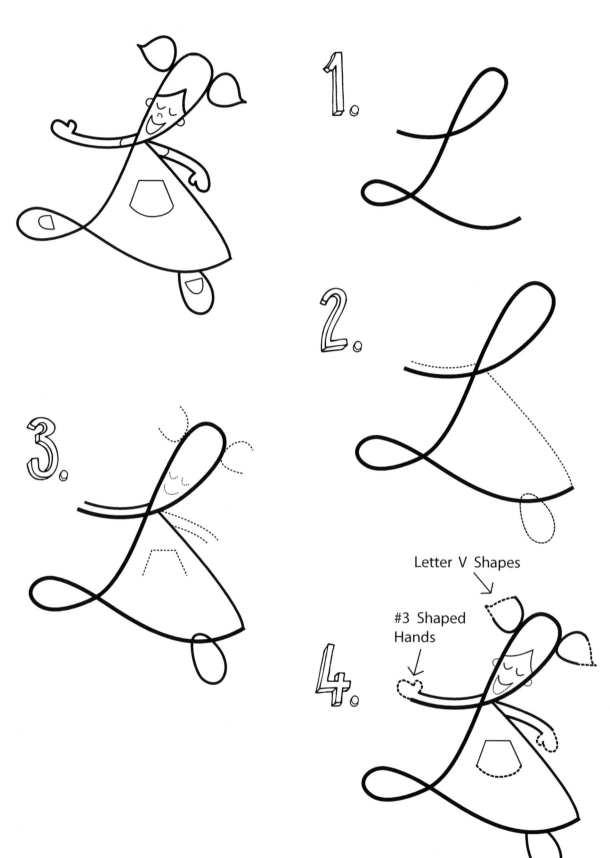

1.

2.

3.

4.

Letter V Shapes

#3 Shaped Hands

5.

Letter D Shapes

↓ NOW YOU TRY ↓

LETTER M SUITED MAN

1. m

2. m

Letter C Nose

3. #5 → Shape

4. #3 Shaped Chin

5. #3 Shaped Tongue →

Letter Y Shape →

6. ← Sideways Letter M Shape

← Letter D Shape

7.

NOW YOU TRY

LETTER N PENGUIN

1.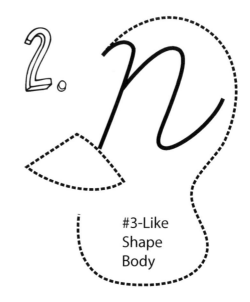

2.

#3-Like
Shape
Body

3.

Letter
M Shape

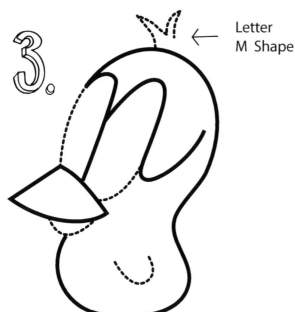

Letter V
Shape

4.

5.

6.

Sideways
Letter V →

NOW YOU TRY

LETTER O PLAYER

1.

Sideways Letter C

2.

3.

Letter L and U Sleeves

4. Letter U and C Shapes

Letter L Shapes

5.

D Shape

#3 Shape

Letter W and U Shapes

6. Letter C Shapes

Letter U Shapes

7.

NOW YOU TRY

LETTER P HORSEY

1. P

2. P

Letter C Shape

Letter M and V Shapes

3. P

Letter C Shaped Nostrils

Letter V and M Shapes

4. P

Letter T Shape

5.

↓ NOW YOU TRY ↓

LETTER Q QUEEN

1. Q

2. Q

Draw the Letter Q Again but in Reverse

Sideways Letter S Shape

3.

4.

5.

6.

#3
Shaped
Tongue

↓ NOW YOU TRY ↓

LETTER Q HEDGEHOG

(There Are Two Letter Q Tutorials Because There Are Two Ways To Write a Cursive Q)

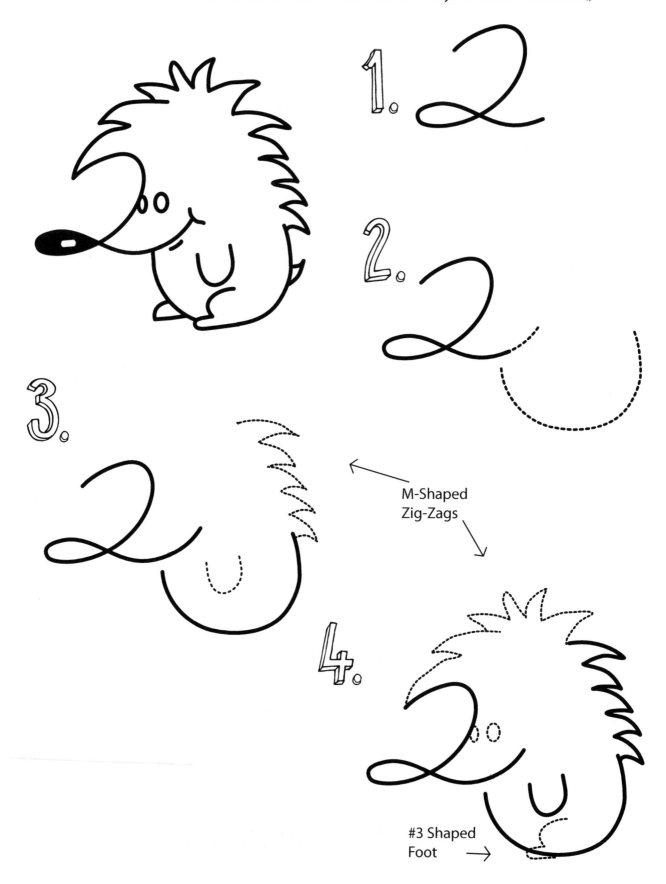

1.

2.

3.

← M-Shaped
Zig-Zags

4.

#3 Shaped
Foot →

5.

Letter V Shaped Tail

Letter D Shaped Foot

↓ NOW YOU TRY ↓

LETTER R RABBIT

1.

2.

Letter D
Shape

3.

Curved
Letter V
Shapes for
Ears

4.

#3
Shape

5.

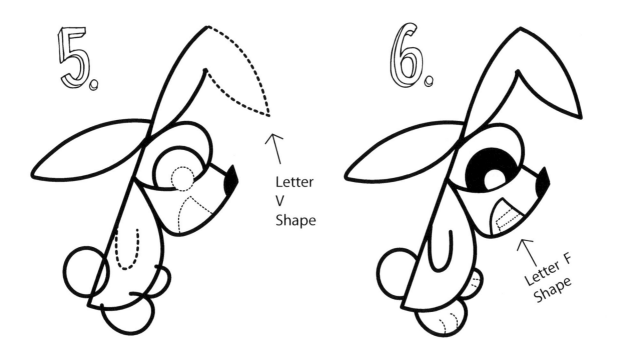

Letter
V
Shape

6.

Letter F
Shape

LETTER S SWAN

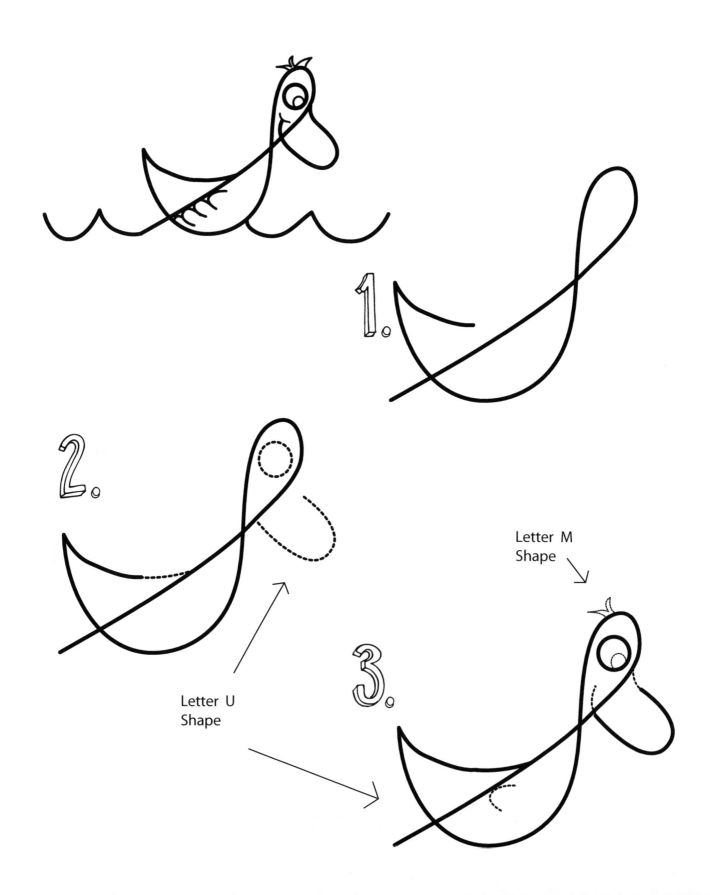

1.

2.

Letter U
Shape

Letter M
Shape

3.

4.

More Letter U Shapes

↓ NOW YOU TRY ↓

LETTER T DOCTOR

1.

2.

3.

4.

Letter M Shapes for Hairs

← Letter Y Shape →

Sideways Letter E Shape ←

5. Letter V Hairs

Letter S in the Ear

Letter D Shapes

Sideways Letter B Shoes

6.

↓ NOW YOU TRY ↓

LETTER U LION

1.

2.

3.

Letter U Shapes

#5 Shape

4.

#8 Shape

#5 and Letter L Shapes

5.

Wiggly Line for the Mane

NOW YOU TRY

LETTER V DEER

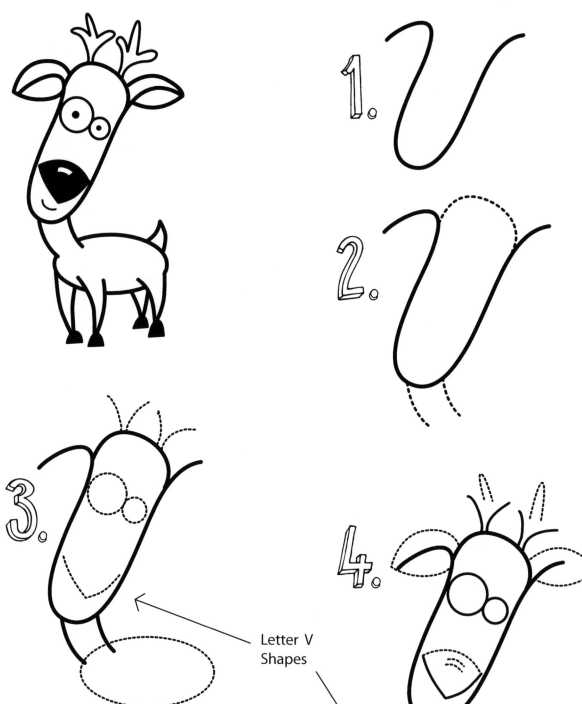

1.

2.

3.

4.

Letter V
Shapes

5.

Letter
D
Shapes

NOW YOU TRY

LETTER w BAT

1.

2.

3.

↑ ↑
#3 Shapes

4.

5.

↓ NOW YOU TRY ↓

LETTER X FISHY

1.

Letter C Shape

2.

#3 shape

3.

4.

Letter V Shapes

5.

Scales on the fish can be drawn
from #3-like humps

6.

NOW YOU TRY

LETTER Y BATHING FLAMINGO

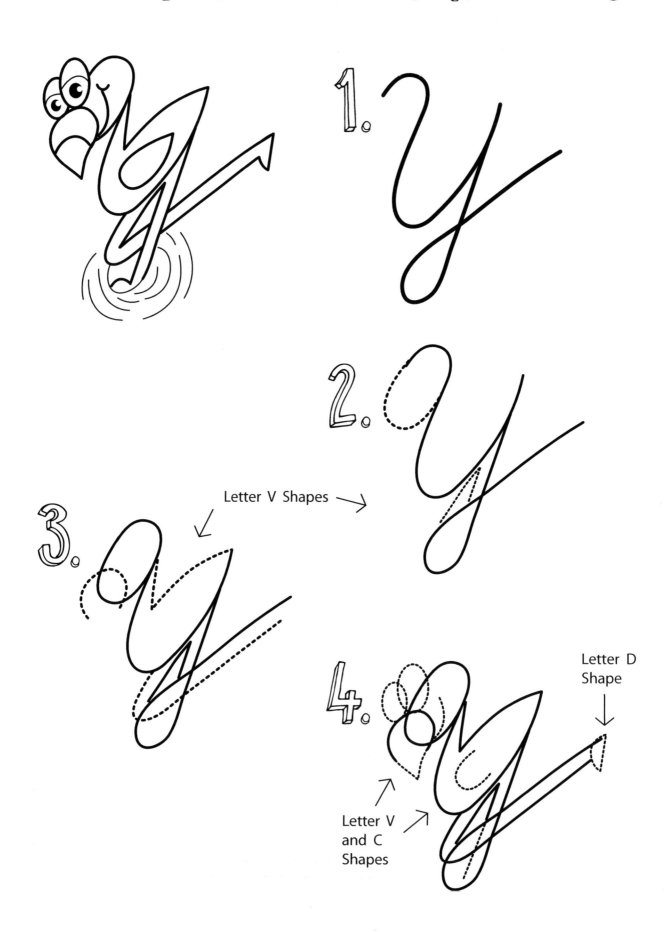

1.

2.

Letter V Shapes →

3.

4.

Letter D Shape

Letter V and C Shapes

NOW YOU TRY

LETTER Z MOUSE

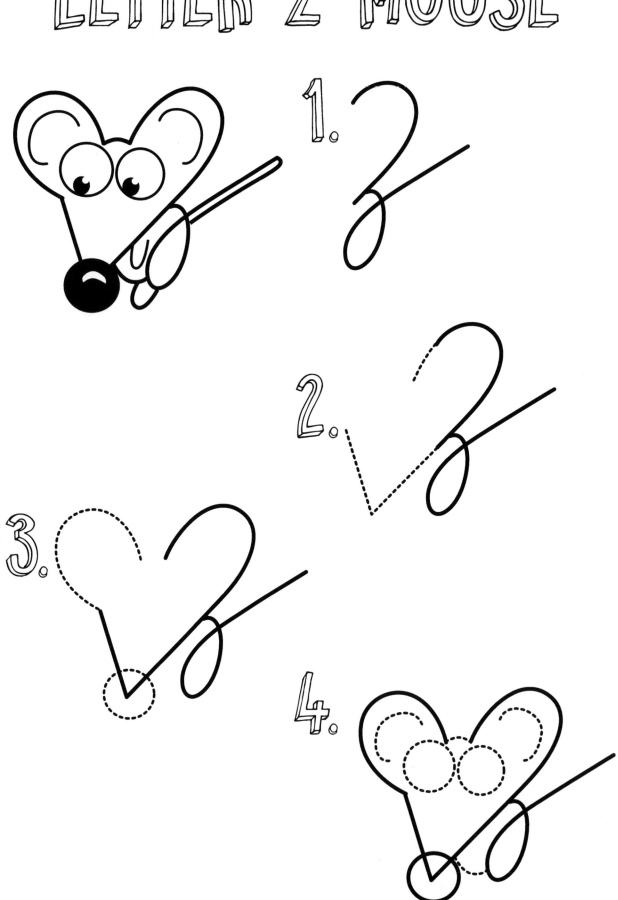

1.

2.

3.

4.

5.

6.

NOW YOU TRY

OUR OTHER BOOKS

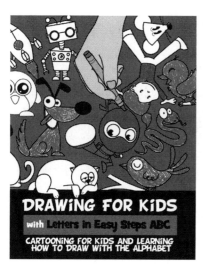

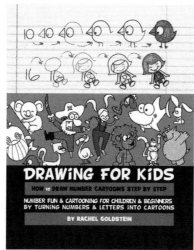

Please Give Us Good Reviews on Amazon!
If You Give us a 5 Star Review, and Email us
About it, We Will Do a Tutorial Per Your
Child's Request and Post it On
DrawingHowToDraw.com

Made in the USA
Middletown, DE
16 June 2021